Silent Sounds

By Richard Jennings

Dedicated to my heart

JK

Dear Reader,

I sincerely hope you enjoy my work, and I would like to thank you for taking your time to read it.

The Silent Sound is a collection of my writing, but it's so much more than that. The true Silent Sound is actually emotion. You may be wondering what this has to do with my writing, but that's just it. That confusion, that's it. The writing made you confused. That's what the writing has to do with it. Emotion affects how we think, how we act, and how we react. Emotion is how we feel, and feeling is great. It shows we're still alive. So if you come away from this, or anything for that matter, without feeling, pinch yourself and make sure you're alive. For those of you with a heartbeat, please let yourself feel as you read. Last but not least, enjoy the ride. :}

Sincerely Yours,
Richard Jennings

About Her

I wanted to write a poem to
Lay it all on the line

But I realized
I wouldn't have the time

Because I have
So damn much to say

I could write you
A poem for days

But I'll keep this one
Short and sweet

And I'll shorten it
By a few feet

I want you to know
You drive me wild

I haven't felt
This way in a while

Your smile's contagious
Like a cold in the rain

Your eyes are a sight
For sore eyes in pain

I wish I could tell you
How I felt

But for now you belong
With somebody else

You'll know who you are
When you hear or read

These lines and I hope
You feel the same for me

All In All

All in all I, fear these wounds, will come alive, and
clear these rooms, of life.

I fear the children with nowhere to go, will all
perish in the snow. Give them blankets keep them
warm; prepare them for the coming storm. They
might not make it; they'll probably die, but for the
children, don't tell them a lie.

All in all I, fear these wounds, will come alive and,
clear these rooms, of life.

I fear the soldiers will take the men, and what will
happen to the women then? Sold to slavers for
silver and gold, take the strong and slaughter the old.
Who do they cry for in their sleep at night?
Someone to save them and make things right.
There's no hero coming to save the day, there's no
savior on the way. So tell the women what you wish,
but I want you to remember this. They'll be forced
to work until they die, but for the women, don't tell
them a lie.

All in all I, fear these wounds, will come alive, and
clear these rooms, of life.

And so the men were left for last, they needed
something and they needed it fast. They need just

one man to make an escape, so comes the conversation were having today. I've got a plan for you, you see; just a plan for you and me. So keep it a secret from all the rest, promise me that you'll do your best. I don't care what you tell them, and don't be shy, but whatever you tell them, make sure it's a lie.

All in all, I fear these wounds, will come alive, and clear these rooms, of life.

Leave me here I beg of you please, I'm suffering from my own disease. I'm going crazy I'm losing my mind, so do me a favor with ties that bind. Leave me here I'll be alright; I'm asking you please to leave me behind. If you're still here and I lose myself, I'll kill you and everyone else. So I'm asking you nicely, one more time, I'm begging you please, just leave me behind.

All in all, I fear these wounds, will come alive, and clear these rooms, of life.

American Tragedy

A drop of blood reflecting a face

The unborn son of the human race

The American dream that was never dreamt

A big white house and a picket fence

But you're stuck with the life you've got

Left in a shithole to die and rot

You've got no money and no reprieve

You've got no cause to sigh in relief

But back to the face that bled from you

It's a reflection of the mirror reflecting you

You're the cast out of the happy

Left to recieve the hand-me down crappy

And the janitor to pick up the mess

While everybody else recieves the rest

You wish for better times to come

But you find that in the land of oppurtunity, there
are none

Black Oz

You're not in Kansas anymore, you're no longer
home

The eyes in the bushes tell you you're not alone

Follow the road of black bricks and stones

To the evil place called the Wizards Dome

Where games are played and lives are lost

Where people are forced to pay the cost

Of one mans greed and one mans lust

The man that goes by the name of Oz

An evil man who lies and cheats

Spilling blood into the streets

The man that feels he can't be beat

So stay light upon your feet

Go to his lair and take the knife

Find the wizard and take his life

Or he'll fill your lungs with smoke and fog

The evil wizard, the wizard of Oz

Blow You Away

Day by day you played the part, but you
haven't impressed me yet. Out of all things
you stole my heart; it's a choice you may
regret. So as we sit here merrily, I've got
something to say. You may think you're
ahead of me, but you're not ahead today.

Cuz I've got a hand in my pocket and one on
the trigger. Pull the other one out to give you
the finger. Take one more shot, to ease the
pain, as I take one too, as I take one too…
blow you away.

Contradicted to Hell

I'm a contradiction like musical silence
Living in a world of peaceful violence

Dug out of the ground like a worthless treasure
Fished from the sea in unnatural weather

Every line can stand alone
The walls of house and home

It all comes toppling down
There's fire the world around

Ash falls from the sky like snow
Rain turns to steam when it hits the stone

I walk on at the break of day
There's no sun in the month of May

This world I'm in it feels so strange
I'm standing at the entrance to Heaven's Gates

This place is not for the likes of me
So I jump and set myself free

Falling through both sky and ground
I end my journey in a world with flames abound

Dead Battery

When the music stops the heart lies still

Someone forgot to pay the bill

The pounding of the drums is the beat of my heart

Ignoring the world is a beautiful art

Fast paced and loud is how I like to live

Play the music out 'til it's got nothing left to give

To the rythm of a heartbeat pounding away

Is the drum of the music refusing to play

Get me to the hospital fast

This heart that isn't built to last

Is giving out and shutting down

Coughing up blood, I'm beginning to drown

In the sounds of the world

And the sight of a girl

Crying in the corner

Hurry up I'm on the border

The battery is dead now charge it up

Blood's leaving my head now a backwards rush

You count it off 1, 2, clear

Soon enough I start to hear

The music's back, I take a breath

Once again, I've escaped death

Deadly Trust

Beware of your gunless friends
They'll only stab you in the back

Betrayal brings friendships to bitter ends
And puts your heart under attack

The deadliest of men is the one you trust
When you're moving forward you never look
behind you

They already know the one thing they must
They already know just where to find you

There's nothing worse than a gunless friend
Quiet kid in the corner with no means to an end

He holds a grudge from days long past
Might've been the times you made him pay for gas

You forgot your money it was an honest mistake
But he's not in the mood for give and take

Like a bottle with no nickel return
That he drinks as the evidence burns

The innocent one now malicious and red
Turned out to be your vicious end

He stabbed you in the back and watched you as you
bled
I said it before and I'll say it again

Don't turn your back on a trusted friend

Existing In Love

If I never existed would you love me the same?
Would I still be the man that you dream of today?
Would I still be the one that takes up your thoughts?
Whether I existed or not?
I'll tell you now this much is true.
I'll never think any different of you.
No matter what, no matter when,
You'll always be the one that I want in the end.

Fade Away

Fade away
Into the darkness that hides the day

The sun starts to crumble into dust
Seeing nothing but blackness because you must

Out of sight out of mind
Fade away for the rest of time

You fade away
Fade away

In the shadows
Under the gallows

The clock is tick tocking
As everyones watching

The rope is tightened around your neck
You try to fight but there's no fight left

As your life begins to fade away
But your legend is here to stay

They took your life and they took your breath
They led you on until your death

Your face is frozen in an endless smile
Because the memory of this will never die

And fade away
Fade away...

Falling Into Your Eyes

I'm lost in a girl
I don't know my way home
Falling off the face of the world
And I'm spiralling out of control

I want you to know
That without you I'd cry
I'm falling off the face of the world in your eyes

I'm falling so hard
Yet I'm falling so softly
All at the same time
I think I'm losing my mind

I love the feeling
When I'm disappearing
I wish I could spend all my time
Getting lost in your eyes

Fighting Time

Flowing time is dripping like a waterfall
Get in line to hit it like a cannonball

It goes on like the rushing of a tidal wave
Left to right like a novel when you turn the page

Time goes on and it waits for no one
Carry on the fight just to show them

Fighting time like swimming against the current
Reading backwards just to learn it

Line for line forever
We go on
Fighting time forever
We go on

So don't stop me now
I'm standing my own ground
As I watch the world go on around me
I was slipping through the distance
Until you came and found me

Now I'm running back to nowhere
The only place you know where
You can find me once again

I'm fighting time I'm swimming against the current
Like reading backwards just to learn it

Line for line forever
We go on

19

Fighting time forever
We go on

Keep on keeping on
We're going on against the dawn

Of a new tomorrow
Without a hope to borrow
But we only hope to beat the sorrow

We carry on
Fighting time against the current
Reading backwards just to learn it
Line for line we carry on
Fighting time we carry on

I wanna know
Will you carry on with me?
Against the current
Carry on with me?
Just to learn it
Carry on with me?

Fighting time together
Line for line forever

Fish like a Poem/Poem like A Fish

I have written these words in black so as to make
them all stand out. They roll from the pencil with
grace, like the smooth swim of a rainbow trout, in a
stream as I cast my line, hoping to catch him so
tonight I may dine.

Otherwise I go hungry in these times that are hard.
There are no buses no stores and no cars. The world
is over, officially now. Some people ask why I
simply ask how.

As I see the fish swim away, with a swim that has
poem like grace, I look at the water that ripples and
sways, and in that water I see a face.

In the water of this broken world, I realize I don't
recognize myself.

Flat Line

I was getting nervous as I awaited your reply
My senses overloading and I thought I could die
That's when I got your message and I looked at
what it said
I had asked you what you felt and what was going
through your head.
Then you wrote "I love you" with a dot dot dot
And I swear to God my heart stopped
That's when my heart stopped beating in my chest
Flat line symphony, that feeling was the best
My body typed the words out that "I love you too"
And if my heart could talk it would say "it's true"

It was almost midnight when I asked you to be mine
To be in a relationship and stand the test of time
That's when you pulled me closer with a smile and
a wink
And then you whispered "yes" and it brought me to
the brink
My heart stopped beating and I nearly fell down
A single tear of joy and I very nearly drown
I held you tighter and I closed my eyes
I thought to myself that I'm a lucky guy

Now I lay on my deathbed with you lying on my
heart
I bid you a due my dear it's time for death to do us
part
We have a love that's so divine
But I know that it's my time
Soon enough you'll fall in line
And the thought makes me smile
Even as I flat line

Forgiveness

Soft knocking at the door
Stepping over the six string on the floor
The white wood swings on its hinges
Answering her silent wishes

He's forgiven the sins of her past
To form a bond that's built to last
He let her in and that was it
Apology accepted and candles lit

Fine food laid out on the table
It seemed unreal like a child's fable
A soft melody she recognized
As their song as she looked in his eyes

Their bodies met in a warm embrace
And his heart began to race
There's no way he could be mad
At a good heart with one blemish of bad

Funhouse Reflection

You tried to mold me to be like you

Teach me to do the things you do

But the message failed in getting through

You thought I was a mirror image

Turns out you're in a funhouse maze

So please don't try to change me

And I'll try not to ruin your day

I've been used and abused

And left black and blue

Changing my shape bruise by bruise

Caught in the wake of what you want

Unwilling and helpless you drag me along

Keeping me going until I drop

Telling me I'm never allowed to stop

I try so hard to make it right

Never putting up a fight

But baby please, I need your help

I need you to let me be myself

Go Ahead and Dance

You must be one with the music let it flow through
your soul
Let it pour from your body through every hole

Shake the dust off your bones and get ready to
dance
If you've never done it before then here's your
chance

Wiggle your hips and move your feet
Dance in your home and dance in the street

Get on down with your bad, bad self
Shake a leg like nobody else

You got the rhythm and you feel the flow
Now I wanna watch you let yourself go

No eyes upon you in your own mind
Dance like you're not from your own time

Freak on a leash you act a fool
From what we see you're looking cool

So get up, dance, and dance some more
Dance yourself right out the door

Dance your way right into the street
You'll be okay if you follow the beat

The rhythm will never lead you astray
As long as you dance the music's way

Has Been

A has been is worse then a never was

I say this simply just because

A never was has dreams and no pain

A has been has memories that drive them insane

So the never was is better off

Because they can't remember what they never lost

The has been's heart is always under attack

Because they want what they can't have back

I'm not going to make an excuse

But my heart feels like it's in a noose

Because I think back to better days

Before this has been's love had gone away

Hold My Hand

Hold my hand
I'll sing you a sweet song
I'll wipe the tears from your eyes

So hold my hand
I'll tell you what you want to hear
Even if it's only lies

They may only be words but they're all we have
Holding us together in the shifting sands

But we're torn apart and we're not alright
So baby please, hold my hand tonight

Home from Heaven is Still Heaven

I feel the need to just let it go
Pick up this pencil and let it flow
Write what comes off the top of my head
Write it down so I don't forget

I tasted a dream but I hit the dawn
The morning dew is on the lawn
It's like spending seven in heaven
When you wished for eleven

I fell from the sky but I lived to tell
I hit the ground before I got to hell
I dust myself off and I start to smile
I haven't been to this place in a while

Home looks the same as it ever did
Coming back again makes me feel like a kid
Memories were so good to me
But I didn't know what good could be

I didn't know but now I do
I only do because of you
And you stand with open arms alone
You stand alone to welcome me home

I Am Not, I Am

I am not a mountain

I am the velvet sky

I am not the horizon

I am the lie

I am not the ocean

I am the sea

I am not the night

I am the breeze

I am not the hero

I am the villian

I am not the victim

I am the one killing

I am not the program

I am the file

I am not the time

I am the while

I am not the story

I am the meaning

I am not the end

I am the beginning

I am not

I just am

Just a Wish Away

I miss you, you know who you are. And you know I can't stand that we're apart. So come home to me now, and I will always be around. I'll always be here. Just call for me now my dear. I'll answer you any time, wether the middle of the day or night. So wait for me today, and I promise I'll find a way, for our bleeding hearts to mend, and we can be together in the end.

King of Ash

I wanna tear down the walls around me
I wanna burn out the fires of hell

I'll erase all written history
Until there's no history to tell

I wanna take the world apart
One city at a time

The time has come for changing
I can see the signs

Bridges burn as time flies by
Ash and smoke fill up the sky

I'm the cause and I'm the reason
For the destruction of the seasons

No more games when blood is spilled
So I reign over the world I've killed

This is a world that's stuck in dead mode
And all that's left is dust and echoes

Leaving Myself Behind

When I'm lost in my ways

And I want to get away

I gotta get on the ship

And I take me a trip

To a better place

Where they don't know my face

They don't know where I've been

Or what I've been in

They won't know who I've loved

And they'll think they know enough

So they'll leave me well alone

I hope you'll miss me when I'm gone

I'm never coming back

Cuz my heart's under attack

They'll love me

For just who I am

Won't try to change me

To make me a better man

I'm gonna go to a place

Where they don't know my face

I'm gonna clean the slates

Gonna forget my mistakes

No longer living in sin

No I'm no longer human

I'm just a shell

My own personal hell

Trying to find who I am

Where do I even begin?

I know where I am

I know where I began

I know what I got

And I know what I want

Midnight at Insanity Square

My mind is a mess, I'm not quite my self

Arguing with my head like I'm somebody else.

Sleepless nights and haunting dreams

Holding back these taunting screams.

Let it out or let myself go

When I decide

I'm sure you'll know

I'm no longer me

and I fear I'll never be.

Love and Other Poisons

We're fighting again and it tears me apart. I fear it's
the end of keeping me in your heart. All I can do is
watch as you walk away, holding back the flood
that will come for days. The door slams and I break
down, I cry myself a river and begin to drown. I
think I need some help from above, because I'm a
prisoner, and I'm dying of love.

So come back through the door and rewind the
scene, to before you gave the poison to me. This
entire movie has been a lie, because everyone
knows the hero never dies. So as we go quickly
back in time, I think of words for the ending lines. I
watch the scene where I begin to fall, and then the
phrase that started it all.

Those three words can be as deadly as poison, "I
love you" means that your life has been shortened.
Cyanide and happiness can not compare, test the
theory if you truly dare. I'm a victim of the
poison above, like I said, I'm dying of love.

But back to the start, where you stole my heart. This
can be seen as the start of the end. For some reason
I don't change the lines, I let it all happen again. I
can't help but to let it go, I don't stop the film I just
let it roll. This is supposed to be the director's cut,
but no edits at all is edit enough. I watch myself as I
fall apart, starting with when you stole my heart. I
watch myself fall to the floor, as you walk out of the
door. Finally it catches up, to exactly what just

happened with us. Watching myself watching
myself, like I'm watching somebody else. I rewind
the film to watch it again. I'm dying of love and I'm
letting it happen.

Mistakes Unbecoming

I'm alone on the field and the stands are all empty

Never enough but there's always plenty

Because I'm alone in this place

This stadium of mistakes

No game to play no one to fight

No I'm not okay no I'm not alright

I'm alone

In this place I've made my home

My mistakes have become my throne

These creations are my own

I'm all alone

Deep from the shadows a mighty roar

Out into the open through the door

A copy of myself made from shadows and hate

He's come to take me to the devil's gate

He's the reason why I'm here

He's the reason why they fear

He's my mistakes all rolled into one

Only one can remain by the time we are done

I pick up the shield and I pick up the knife

Suddenly this stadium bursts into life

Nobody wants to watch you kill someone else

But the story is different when you're killing yourself

There's nowhere to run nowhere to hide

The battle rages on the inside

There's only ourselves to blame ourselves to fight

When the stadium comes to life

I slayed my demon to a roaring crowd

But now I stand with no one around

I'm alone

In this place I've made my home

My mistakes have become my throne

These creations are my own

I'm alone

But through the ground comes the souls of the slain

From the spots where their bodies have lain

But silence echoes through my head

Memories of the forgotten dead

Left here alone until they died

For the entertainment of those who lied

Our demons are beaten

Our past is defeated

But now we are stuck

Shit out of luck

But at least we are not alone in being alone

My Salvation

I know that I'm just a romantic fool,
Sitting at the bottom of a drowning pool,
Filled to the brim by my own tears,
Each one a reflection of my own fears.
I stare up at the light coming from above,
Giving me hope that I've learned to love.
I swim to the top and I break surface.
Before me sits a sight so perfect,
That when I open my eyes I lose the breath I just
caught.
I would speak but my throat becomes a knot.
I swim to shore already knowing what to do,
I give it a kiss because my salvation is you.

On The Rock of Love

Burning hearts like shining stars
Can't remember who we are

Space station floating up above
As we sit on the rock of love

Watching the stars as we spin
On a rock without a wind

Not much to do when you're on the moon
But enjoy the company of me and you

If peace and quiet is a capital crime
I'm happy to be doing time

Listening to Pink Floyd play us a tune
As we sit on the dark side of the moon

Rearview Reflection

I see your eyes in the rearview
But you're watching the road
I've been hiding how I feel
So you wouldn't know
You're too busy paying attention
To notice my reflection
But that's okay
I don't mind it anyway
I love the way you look tonight
Underneath the soft moonlight
Things be awkward if you knew
But I hope that you feel it too
As I watch your eyes in the rearview

Revolution Rock

As thunder rips across the sky
We'll let out an electric cry

The guitars will howl and the drums will slam
Our sound will play across the land

Head bangers anthem a call to arms
Bring them down with drums and guitars

Our voices will cry out toward their wall
And all they know will tremble and fall

Like a phoenix from the ashes
Rise again to move the masses

Metal, Rock, Grunge, and Emo
Punk, Classic, Hardcore, Screamo

We shall rise again to power
Gaining strength with every hour

Head bangers anthem a call to arms
Play our anthem with drums and guitars

Tremble and shake the very foundations
We can unite every nation

Come out of our hiding places
Play our music in their faces

We faded once but never again
Infecting women, children, and men

Nowhere to hide, nowhere to run
Have no fear we've just begun

Head bangers anthem a call to arms
Build this dream on drums and guitars

Bands play storms across the sky
We gather towards the battle cry

In the front stands one lone man
He leads the charge with mic in hand
United by a dream the army stands
Playing as a giant band

A song of freedom a song of heart
They knew the tune right from the start

From the bowels of Hell to the Heaven's above
Fill the land with Rock and love

Head bangers anthem a call to arms
Here because this dream is ours

Like a phoenix from the ashes
We rose again and moved the masses

Zeroes to heroes once before
Zeroes to heroes forevermore

A people united we stand proud
A song of freedom we play out loud

We stand together, we stand free
United we stand, because of a dream

Risen Like the Dead

Deeper words and hidden meanings

Something about new beginnings

Our words are indefinable

Our minds are unreliable

Our dreams are all frayed and scattered

Scope of reality is shattered

We are oh so dazed and confused

We are the ones that always lose

Pushed and pulled down to the ground

Not enough just to push us around

Covered in mud and drenched in blood

You wipe your eyes to stop the flood

They kick us when we're down

To keep us from getting up

They would rather watch us drown

Than hear us say we've had enough

So it's time to take a stand

Against all they're for

Don't bother to knock

Just knock down the door

Now our time has come to get our revenge

They can watch us rise as if from the dead

The bloodied and battered, broken and beat

Get off your backs and onto your feet

We will make them hear our pleas

We'll take our fight into the streets

No rest for the wicked

Or so we'll prove

Cause we've got a reason

And nothing to lose

So follow close our time has come

They'll be like us by the time we're done

They will know what we've been through

And they'll hear us tell them what they're due

They'll ask why how and who

And we'll answer:

YOU

Rockabye Lullaby

Rockabye baby on the treetop, when the wind blows
the cradle will rock. I pray for that cradle to reach
the sky, and sweet little baby will never cry. Baby's
heart will be full for as long as I live, I've got so
much love to give. So rockabye baby I bid you adue,
and I pray that sweet dreams come to you.

Sabotage Salute

Tick tock goes the clock
Counting down the days

I can hear the people talk
Talking about the ways

The ways that we've been beaten
Misused and mistreated

Tensions build up to the point where it's all about to
blow
People won't know what to do where to hide or
where to go

Tick tock goes the counter on the bomb
Under the masses of those who think they do no
wrong

The ticking's not the only sound
There's the heartbeats in our chests
As we're waiting for the moment
There would be nothing left

But a terrible miscalculation
Leads me to the speculation
That soon I'll have no circulation

I have no chance to cross the line
I'd never make the run in time
The bomb strapped to my back about to blow
The clock ticks one to let me know

I'm sitting here the end is near
And I'm about to die
I've got nothing left to do
But kiss my ass goodbye

Sailor Sin

I'm the captain of this ship
I call her lady luck
You say I'm unoriginal
But I say you just suck
These seven drunken sailors
Are the seven deadly sins
They brought you to their leader
That must make me him
I am the king of the seas
That no one wants to sail
Walk the plank off of my ship
Into the sea of Hell

I'm the captain of the sins
Everywhere there is, I've been
Making love to my maidens, tonic and gin
Throwing up in the sea before I push you in
I'm a horrible man
And I don't give a damn
Some before have called me crazy
But I can't be, I'm too lazy
Salty Sailor
Seaborne Jailor
I am the king of the seas
And I do what I please
I am bad for my own health
But I don't care because I'm the king of Hell

Schizophrenic Breakdown

I am the single owner of several souls
They say my mind has got a few holes

I'm not the kind of crazy who hears pointless noises
I'm the kind that talks to bodiless voices

I look in the mirror afraid of what I'll see
Every time I look it's a brand new me

I shatter the glass with a shaky hand
I take a deep breath as I struggle to stand

I stare at the pieces, into my own eyes
Each reflection's worth a thousand lies

Break a piece to kill the image
To create another, with more lies in it

I close my eyes and a tear drop falls
My silent screams echo down the halls

I need to get out and break myself free
But it's impossible to free myself from me

My fears confirmed when I reach for the door
Fade to black as my face meets the floor

So Far

You don't make it as far as I've come without
getting a little dirty, and you can't get what I've got
by shakin' hands. Everybody's got their own worst
enemies, enemies they wish they never had. Smiles
won't buy you time, and words won't make you
strong. Because smiles can be evil, and words can
come out wrong. So don't rely on looks, and don't
put your faith in charm. Because looks can be
decieving, from those who mean you harm.

So Tell Me

What drives you on? Gives you the push to do what
you do?
What's your inspiration, your light in the dark
shining through? Tell me; what's your inspiration,
you driving force? What keeps you working like a
horse?

Is it me? The reason you breathe? Why do you try
so hard? Do you really think you'll get very far?
Raise the par, beat the par? But why? And don't
you dare lie.

So tell me, what is your inspiration? I'm dying to
know. What's your inspiration? For the feelings you
show? So tell me, and don't lie. I hope I'm yours,
because maybe, you are mine.

So tell me, what's your inspiration?

Something to Miss You By

Do me a favor and give me a kiss

Give me a little something to miss

Because I can't stand when you go away

So give me a kiss that will last for days

Make me dream of happier times

When all that matters is you and I

With you in my arms and the sun in the sky

And all that matters is you and I

So baby give me something to miss you by

Stormy Night

I keep on tossing and turning
Rolling around like my bed is burning

I can't sleep and it's four in the morning
For the past few days the weather's been storming

Every so often I see a flash
Seconds later a thunder crash

I sit on my bed alone in the dark
I wonder to myself as to where you are

It's a pain to be so far apart
But I knew the cost and I gave you my heart

I think of the place where we used to meet
And walk on the grass in our bare feet

We used to sing every song
Because we knew every line

We would walk along
Just wasting time

How were we to know
That it wouldn't last

We both said forever
But forever went so fast

So I sit and wait out the night
Wishing you were in my arms tonight

The Other End of the Line

He's forgiven everything you've ever done, but this
mistake is the only one, that he just can't let go. As
he wondered what could be going on, on the other
end of your telephone. You were telling lies that
you thought he would believe, but you were soon to
find that he's not easy to decieve.

So he found out what you've done, and now he's
holding a loaded gun, and even though he hates
himself for it, it's the smartest thing that he ever did.
Two shots each right through the heart, two shots to
tear love apart. All because of what you've done,
when you lied on the telephone.

Holes in paper nailed to a tree, pictures hanging of
you and me. He took two shots each right through
the heart, two shots to tear paper hearts apart. And
even though he hates himself for it, it's the smartest
thing he ever did, to leave those pictures in the rain,
and forgive the mistake that you've made.

So as he sits and he wonders what's going on, on
the other end of your telephone, tell him the truth
and you will be free, from having your picture
nailed to a tree.

The Sheppard: Rock 'N' Roll

Stop all the clocks
Get ready to go

The crowd is a flock
The Sheppard: Rock 'N' Roll

Guitar is thunder through the midnight sky
The drum is a heartbeat refusing to die

The music rips the silence of night
For miles around there's people in sight

Hearts race as the volume grows
There's no need for columns and rows

The crowd is as one
Shaking the Earth

They felt the call
Since the moment of birth

Nothing to do and nowhere to go
Brought together by Rock 'N' Roll

The World in Your Eyes

Imagine a place where the grass is green

With the smell of roses riding the breeze

Flowers of yellow like the sun in the sky

A sea of green like the sea in your eyes

The trees grow tall with initials carved

Reminding us just who we are

The waves of the ocean crash on the rocks

Telling the time like the hands of a clock

No need for clocks when father time doesn't care

Mother Nature's breeze flows through your hair

We feel no pain and we have no need

As we lock eyes beneath the trees

Walking closer you keep the gaze

Embrace each other like the Sun's warm rays

Find happiness in each others arms

In a world that could do no harm

And as we get lost in this beautiful world

This boy gets lost in a beautiful girl

Look in his eyes and enjoy the view

This boy only wants to tell you he loves you

These Lights

Shaking, vibrating, buzzing, and shining.
Oh my God these lights keep whining.
Rip them out and take them please
Get these lights away from me

They watch me work and they watch me play
They watch and watch all night and day

As I wait and watch the clock tick
Under these lights I feel like I'm sick

When they're on me I can't focus
They shut me off like hocus pocus

The buzz of these lights drives me insane
They mess with my head and confuse my brain

They stop up the process of thought
Lead me to believe things that are not

It's a conspiracy, I think at least
The buzzing itself becomes its own beast

I crave to get up and flip the switch
But the teacher would pitch a fit

So I sit here suffering and quiet
Listening to lights on an electric diet

The War of A Single Soldier

Another day another night
Preparing for another fight
Checking weapons loading guns
Attacking with the rising sun
From dawn til dusk and dusk til dawn
The single soldier struggles on
Against himself and his own mind
Trying to leave himself behind
To forget the life that he once lived
The very life he chose to give
Traded for the lives he took
But backwards is the way he can not look
He can't stand to let himself see
The man that he let himself be
So the single soldier struggles on
Trying his hardest to forget
The memories that he left behind
Thankful they haven't caught him yet

Truth on a Blank Page

Deeper words and hidden meanings
Something about new beginnings

The answers trapped on an empty page
Unwritten words of lyrical rage

Search my words for some kind of proof
To show yourself a bogus truth

Interpreting this will lead to a lie
Because the meaning is plain to the eye

It is as it says but it speaks in tongues
You won't understand even after I'm done

You read my lines then stop to think
As I push you toward the brink

Of unspeakable sadness
Brought on by my lyrical madness

My mind is of profanity
Simply proving my insanity

Sign of a genius is a mess
Give me the best forget the rest

For the gift to write I do feel blessed
But when I'm done I won't know what's left

My words are fuel to a raging fire
As the gasses take us higher

That line had nothing to do with anything at all

But I'm here to catch you when you fall

It will happen, don't say no
Because I'm not gonna let you go

Over the edge like many before
I took the key and locked the door

As I said my words have no meaning
This poem was crap from the beginning

Unsure

Wait for me I won't give in

Even if I'm sure I can't handle it

I'm not sure why but I'm sure I know

One day we'll find somewhere to go

I'm not sure but I think it's because

I'm not sure of myself but I'm sure of us

You're the one thing I've always been sure about

Even if I'm just pushing the word around

The word love often comes to mind

But sometimes I wonder if I'm blind

Because I can't see what you can see

Or the reason that you're in love with me

The mirror lies as it speaks in tongues

But not knowing the truth is half the fun

I'm not sure why and I'm sure it's because

I'm not sure of myself but I'm sure of us

You're the one thing I've always been sure about

Even if I'm just pushing the word around

So step right up introduce me to myself

Say hello to me like I'm somebody else

Let me know all that I've missed

And kiss this boy like he's never been kissed

Take your time there's no need for haste

Take your time let me savor the taste

Of your lips on mine when they connect

Let me dial your number and I'll call collect

From the payhone down the street

Hoping maybe we could meet

To bring this restless wait to an end

And I can feel your kiss again

Velvet Infinity

In a sky made out of velvet there's a sun that shines
like gold
The light you give me brightens up my soul

Because there's a skyline of velvet and smoke on
the horizon
You set my heart on fire without even trying

I jump off the edge of the world into my own trust
Because where I land there's nothing else but us

And with a skyline of velvet and a sun that shines
gold
We're left here together where love never gets old

Walk a Mile

Keep me warm in the fires of truth

I've been reborn from the ashes of youth

Reality consists of twisted lies

A connected world of broken ties

It's all about the show

The words dont mean anything anymore

All of a sudden a blast from the past

And everything we know goes out the door

A sudden reminder of who we are

We've got miles to go without a car

Walk a mile in a wise man's shoes

And then you'll learn to sing the blues

You will know the value of pain

As you're walking in the rain

Move your feet forever more

Never knowing what's in store

Move your feet because you must

In the confusing story of us

Waiting

I made you a promise to be here forever
So here I stand through every weather

I told you I would be forever strong
Who knew forever would take so long?

I'm wearing down right to the bone
I've lost my body I'm just a soul

Yet I still stand here forever true
Hoping I can make it up to you

Forgive me for the promise that binds me here
And keeps me away from you my dear

You move on and live your life
I'm stuck in stone like Arthur's knife

As I stand I look back again
To a time when I wasn't a man

But a boy who didn't know
what to say or how to show

The feelings for you that made him blush
And that first kiss was such a rush

And when I held you in my arms
I felt the world could do no harm

But I am stuck here all alone
Without your heart to call a home

Like a hand waiting for a dove
I wait forever for your love

But as time keeps raging on
I stand as a soul, my body gone

I can't do much but I do what I can
So I wait for you with outstretched hand

We Take Strays

Driving down a littered highway

Life just wasn't going my way

I saw a sign at the break of day

It said we take strays

I get inside I hear a baby

I see an old man and a little lady

A cozy place with a fire by the wall

I gave them my name and asked how much I owed
her

Pulled my money out and showed her

She said I didn't owe a thing

She said it's okay

Because we take strays

We gathered downstairs for dinner

Everyone everywhere is a sinner

It doesn't matter in this place

Used to be a guitar for hire

Inspired by the six string by the fire

I took that six string out of its case

I sang we take strays

From all directions

We take strays

With no selection

We take strays

From all directions

We take strays

I left that place after a while

The good folks sent me with a smile

Wished me many happy days

And they said please remember, we take strays

What's Best For Me

My scars show white right through the dark
The darkness of your empty heart

I know it will take a while
But I won't stand here and fake a smile

I found my way away from you today
To a place where I could stay

Everything you said has been a lie
Everything else just meant goodbye

I'm leaving you behind
So I can keep you off my mind

When you loved me and I loved you
I knew it was too good to be true
But now I've got all of the proof
There's only one thing for me to do

Cry a river, build a bridge, and get over it.

Will You?

What if I can't take it? What if it leaves me weak?
Will you be my hero, the protector of the meek?
Will you stick up for me? When I can't defend
myself? Will you come and save me, from all the
depths of hell? I guess what I'm really asking, and I
hope this isn't a bad time, is would you make me
happy? Would you like to be mine?

Your Ex

Like a liar weaving webs fornicating with the truth

Who whispers evil thoughts into the ears of youth

But you can't read the lines he's trying to use

Everytime he's lying to you

But I guess you're blind to the fact

That your ex-boyfriend doesn't love you back

So why do you stick around? I know you see what he's trying to do.

I'm not that dumb and neither are you

But I start to question if you're really worth it

If I should keep fighting or if I should forfeight

Because you're still in love with your ex-boyfriend

Though you were only his means to an end

And I feel like I'm being forgotten

Because I see when we're talking

That you're thinking of him

So I sit waiting patiently

For something you can wait and see

Soon enough they'll start to sprout

And his true colors will come pouring out

But you won't believe me yet again

And you'll tell me he's your best friend

Because you're still in love with your ex-boyfriend

Though you were only his means to an end

And I feel like I'm being forgotten

Because I see when we're talking

That you're thinking of him

And maybe one day you will see

And on that day you come running to me

I will be waiting to make you my own

I will make sure that you're never alone

And I will treat you like a queen

Because that's how much you mean to me

But for now

You're still in love with your ex-boyfriend

Though you were only his means to an end

And I feel like I'm being forgotten

Because I see when we're talking

That you're thinking of him

Winter Dreaming

As the day drags on so slow
I stare out the window into the snow
I dream of snowmen kids and sleds
Longing for hot drinks movies and bed
Waiting for the final bell
Driveways to shovel service to sell
As I walk home I'm all alone
But in the snow all fear is gone
Sheer beauty, so soft and white
As it falls it reflects the light
Back from my head I do return
Back to the season of sun and burns
For now my dreams are slightly hindered
As I long for the joys of winter

Overboard

Man overboard! I'm going in to save my self
tonight.
The storm is coming fast, and I've got to get this
right.
This is the nightmare, I've been fighting, so that
it would not come true,
but I could not keep this dream from you.
So trust me now, I'll get us out, I'll carry you to
shore. Life boats are gone, I carry on,
I swim forever more.
I am the man, man overboard.
I swim forever more.

Sink or swim I'll do my best.
Just hold on tight I'll do the rest.
No hope if there's no faith,
So believe in me and we'll be safe.
Oh, I can't believe I couldn't see, that you could
share this dream with me.
Now it's got us both, and we've got no boat, but
we've got each other we're not alone.
Time to save my soul I'm going in
I'm learning fast it's sink or swim

Man overboard! I'm going in to save my self
tonight.
The storm is coming fast, and I've got to get this
right.
This is the nightmare, I've been fighting, so that
it would not come true,
but I could not keep this dream from you.
So trust me now, I'll get us out, I'll carry you to
shore. Life boats are gone, I carry on,
I swim forever more.

I am the man, man overboard.
I swim forever more.

Man overboard! I'm going in to save my self
tonight.
The storm is coming fast, and I've got to get this
right.
I swim forever more.
I am the man, man overboard.
I swim forever more.
I am the man, man overboard.

The sky is getting dark
I can feel your beating heart
The water's oh so cold
and it keeps getting up your nose
and you can't stand the thought
of wether we'll make it or not
but I'm gonna tell you, you shouldn't worry, and
if we don't make it, I'm truly sorry. But I've got
a feeling and I hope you feel it too, so don't give
up on me and I'll never quit on you. I'll be the
savior you've been waiting for. So forgive my
behavior, I know you wanted more.
So hold on tightly I'll keep fighting, through the
rain and all the lightning.
And even if I drown, just know that I will never
let you down.
I swim forever more.
The savior you've been waiting for.
Man overboard.

Man overboard! I'm going in to save my self
tonight.
The storm is coming fast, and I've got to get this
right.

This is the nightmare, I've been fighting, so that
it would not come true,
but I could not keep this dream from you.
So trust me now, I'll get us out, I'll carry you to
shore. Life boats are gone, I carry on,
I swim forever more.
I am the man, man overboard.
I swim forever more.

Man overboard! I'm going in to save my self
tonight.
The storm is coming fast, and I've got to get this
right.
I swim forever more.
I am the man, man overboard.
I swim forever more.

Man overboard! I'm going in to save my self
tonight.
The storm is coming fast, and I've got to get this
right.
This is the nightmare, I've been fighting, so that
it would not come true,
but I could not keep this dream from you.
So trust me now, I'll get us out, I'll carry you to
shore. Life boats are gone, I carry on,
I swim forever more.
I am the man, man overboard.
I swim forever more.

All My Dreams Are Nightmares

Sweet dreams are just some words
And sleep is a dream I can't afford
Because all my dreams are nightmares
And it's time to sleep if I dare

But at night I face my demons
At night they come to life
And when I'm waking up then I know everything's
alright

No I'm not okay
And no you can not help
Because this is a problem I have got to face myself

Because all my dreams are nightmares
And it's time to sleep if I dare
I close my eyes
And I cross the line
And my dreams become the truth
But I keep dreaming of you
But you're gone away
Oh so far away
So my dream becomes a nightmare
And I'm not quite sure if I care

And sweet dreams are just some words
Because sleep is a dream I can't afford
Because all my dreams are nightmares
But it's time to sleep if I dare

And at night I face my demons
At night they come to life
And when I'm waking up I know that everything's
alright

No I'm not okay
And no you can not help
Because this is a problem I have got to face myself

The inside of my eyelids
Remind me of what I did
When I told you those words
The words you never heard

And so you walked away
From what we could have had
And you left me standing
Back where we began
Way back when you gave up
And I can't wake up
And all my dreams are nightmares
All my dreams are nightmares
And they're true
Because I dream of you

And sweet dreams are just some words
And sleep is a dream I can't afford
Because all my dreams are nightmares
But it's time to sleep if I dare

I don't dare
I can't face myself tonight
But I don't care
Because I've got to get this right
Replay the moment
Up in my head
Rewind it way back
To the time when
I let you go
And you didn't know

All my dreams are nightmares
All my dreams are true
Because my only nightmare
Is when I'm losing you
So I can't stand to sleep
Because I see you in my dreams
And we won't make up
But I can't wake up
So kill me now
And let me out

Because all my dreams are nightmares
And it's time to sleep if I dare
But sweet dreams are just some words
And sleep is a dream I can't afford
But tonight I face my demons
Tonight they come to life
Because I'm gonna call you
And make everything alright
I'll tell you what I should have
Oh so long ago
The words I tried to tell you
The ones you didn't know

So tonight I face my demons
Tonight they come to life
Because I'm gonna call you
And make everything alright

And sweet dreams are just some words
And sleep is a dream I can't afford
Because all my dreams are nightmares
And it's time to sleep if I dare

No I'm not okay
And no you can not help
Because this is a problem I have got to face myself

Because all my dreams are nightmares
All my dreams are nightmares
All my dreams are nightmares
And they're true
Because I dream of you

Bullets and Flames

Your eyes are the skies and they're burning through
my skin
My heart is crying out to me that I should let you in
But every time I do you always make it rain
But I take the risk, bite the bullet, feed the flame
Because you're worth the fire and all the Hell
Let you through my outer shell
I'll bite the bullet and save my life
Feed the flame and forge the knife
To kill the fear of an aching heart
That's exactly where I should start
But I'm just a kid
I'm not that smart
So I let you in, young and reckless
And I'm happy, in love and restless
Bite the bullet, feed the flame
So I can hear you say my name

Here for You

This one's coming from way down deep
It's about the reason that I can't sleep
I decided to write you a poem
To say that I'm not in pain I'm just alone
I hate waiting when I'm confused
Especially when there's nothing that I can do
Because I hate it when you're not okay
And I can't stand when you're in pain
I can't help it and I can't help myself
From wishing there was some way I could help
But I will never go astray
I'll be here for you forever starting today

Afraid of the Dark

You wanna scream but there's nobody there
Even if they were they wouldn't care
It's a childish fear that you should've let go
They don't understand, no, nobody knows
The reason why you need a light
Just so you can get some sleep at night

In your head there's a dark tomorrow
A world that's drowned in sadness and sorrow
The pain inside your burning heart
Is the reason that you find that you're afraid of the
dark

Like a child it's all in your head
You keep a night light next to your bed
No you can't stand to be alone
Even in the walls of your own home

It's a nightmare that comes to life
When you can't sleep without a light
Sit up in your bed with a hand on a knife
Hoping you can find a way to fight the night

In your head there's a dark tomorrow
A world without a path to follow
Confusion in your head overpowers your heart
That's the reason that you find that you're afraid of
the dark

You were never brave and never bold
Paranoia sets in like a cold
Every little sound becomes a brand new threat
Sleep is just a dream that you'll regret

In your head there's no tomorrow
A world without a hope to borrow
The fear in your head instilled in your heart
Is the reason that you find that you're afraid of the
dark

Avenging Agent

Sleep eat read keep
Secrets that you won't believe
Wasting time by telling lies
Line by line the seconds die
A perfect stranger with a smile
Gives some thought for a little while
Walking down the city street
And your feet move to the beat
Paces change you move along
But the rhythm's going strong
Sitting watching taking notes
Watch him reach into his coat
Pulls a gun out from his vest
Two shots put right through his chest
The stranger falls down in the dark
Of course you always hit the mark
You're a secret agent trained in death
Check his vitals there's no breath
Flash the badge calm the crowd
For some strange reason they hang around
A crew shows up to clean the mess
And you go home to get some rest

Flew the Coupe

Sitting in the corner
Watching time go by
Tell you what you wanna hear
I'm always telling lies
I sit and watch the time tick by
Staring at the clock
Chained down to the desk
Under key and lock
I'm a beast, an outcast
Monster of my own design
Psychotic and insane
In between I walk the line
Writing and writing
Put the pencil to the paper
Grind the pencil to the metal
And then the tip is tapered
Use it to pick the lock
And secure my freedom
They told me lies
And tried to force me to believe them
If they try to stop me
They will fail like all the rest
They will find already gone
This cuckoo, flew the nest

Handsome Devil

Handsome devil with a charming smile
But I beg of you don't fall in love with me
I'll say yes because it's been a while
And turn you into what you don't wanna be
Easy to fall in love with hard to forget
You'll never know it but I'm a choice you'll regret
So run from me now don't ever ask why
If you start to wonder just keep this in mind
I'm a poison, I'm a curse
If love is the path I walk reverse
So run, run as fast as you can
And pray I don't catch you; I don't know who I am

Letter to Love Lost

I love you. You know that. I'd die for you at the
drop of a hat. I don't know much, but what I do
hurts my heart. And I can't fix it because I'm busy
tearing myself apart. I was thinking of writing you a
letter, but thought to myself that I could do better.
I'm happy for you. I really am. And I want to show
it but I don't know if I can. Because it hurts, I'm not
gonna lie. I guess I'm jealous you're with another
guy. I hope you can forgive me, this isn't what I
wanted. I never meant to upset you, but I've got to
be honest. Seeing you happy with somebody else,
and thinking I could have done it better myself. I
can't help the way I feel, but somehow I've got to
deal. I would love to let you in. But this tour guide
doesn't know where to begin.

Lost Love's Road

There's so many things that I would like to
remember
But somehow my mind is set to forget
And as I walk on in this never-ender
Not saying goodbye is my only regret
I miss the thought, the sight, and the smell
I miss everything I can no longer have
I pause for a moment so I can tell
The wind is to my back
I walk on roads of sorrow
I fly on wings of gold
Searching for tomorrow
Forever on lost love's road

Seductive Stress Reliever

She's one hell of a way to ease the stress

Because she's dynamite in a party dress

And she really knows how to dance

So if you're up to take a chance

Place your bet and let it rip

Buy her a drink and take a sip

She's the type to always say yes

And she's dynamite in a party dress

So take her home and take it off

She's a loaded bomb that's ready to drop

So light the fuse and watch it burn

Stare at the flame as she does a turn

She's ready to go lock and load

Careful now she's set to explode

Tears and Fears

You can't fight the tears that won't come

And you can't chase the fear that won't run

When you're trading one for the other

You end up with another

Now your head is a mess

And you're feeling the stress

But you can't break free

From the catastrophe

That's become you

And all that you can do

Is cry

And try

To set your fear free through your eyes

But you can't fight the tears that won't come

And you can't chase the fear that won't run

The 3 Words You're 2 Afraid 2 Say

On the phone for an hour already
Trying to breathe but your chest is heavy
Words unspoken weighing down
Bleeding heart beginning to drown
The three words you're too afraid to say
But you don't know any other way
So you ask if I meant what I said
And I told you that I did
Somehow my words killed the fear
And you whispered in my ear
That you meant the same
And set my heart aflame
Like the passion in your eyes
But your eyes are the skies
Burning through my skin
Forcing me to let you in
Because there is no other way
Than the three words you're too afraid to say

The Darker Path

Bullies only made me stronger
Haters only give me strength
Come on baby push me harder
I'm going the entire length
All the way, day or night
Everyday, do or die
Bite the bullet, feed the flame
Pull the trigger hear the bang
Body falls, bite the dust
Dull the edge on the knife that cuts
Across the skin it starts to bleed
Reminding me of what I need
I'm not sure if you even can
But I need you to remind me who I am
Someone to help me do the math
Put me back on the brighter path
Keep me from turning into a liar
Before I walk into the fire

To the Rhythm of a Rooftop Romance
It could be criminal

The way you move

Hypnosis

They way you catch the groove

Entrancing

As the moonlight falls

The music is sweet

The moment stalls

Keeping itself alive

For you and I

I dare not take the chance

Because I know that I can't dance

It could be criminal

You and I

Because us

Is killing time

But it's oh so sweet

The way you move your feet

Towards where I placed my chair

So close I can smell your hair

Lean in and whisper

Without any words

Because your kiss

It's all I heard

And your rhythm

All I felt

I catch your groove

Begin to melt

You pull me slowly from the seat

And show me how to move my feet

You gave me all the proof

And showed me an undeniable truth

I learned to dance

With you on that roof

To the rhythm of a romance

Beneath the moon

Wingless Angel

Gonna go do what I do best. Go for a walk and be depressed. So forget the sun and the moon in the sky. I'll never reach them because this angel can't fly. Stuck on the ground with nothing but a beat. But I can't even dance, I got cement on my feet. So I'm gonna sit here and write until I can't anymore. Then I'll stand up and kick my self out the door.

Beat myself up because I deserve it. Just because I want to hurt him. Depressed and pissed off and I'm not sure which. A little bit of both with neither dominant. Speaking how I feel because I just don't care. And if there's a problem the door's over there. I'm not gonna sit quiet and play the victim. The old me didn't leave the party, I kicked him. That's a gamer joke you'll never understand. Because I won't explain myself again.

Talk is cheap so I won't. And acting is lying so I don't. I'm messed up and depressed, this feeling's the best. And I don't want to be cured not now not ever. This is how I am, messed up forever. So stuff me in a cage but don't lock it up. I'm not leaving anyway I'm stuck in a rut. Just gonna sit in my own misery. Because it always gets the best of me. And every single time, I always find, I lose control. Because deep down inside, I'm an asshole.

Ghost in the Corner

Kid in the corner who nobody knows
What would it be like if I were a ghost?
Tell me, can you see me?
Do you notice?
I'm invisible, one with the shadows
Silently viewing a world so shallow
I see what you don't want me to see
Because you never notice me
I'm always watching, always there
And you never know because you never care
But it doesn't bother me, it never will again
Because I become a God when I pick up a pen
Control the world with every word
Write you to death, end the world
Bring it back, do it again
Throw the page in the trash in the end
But you'll never know
Because you can't see the show
But can you see me?
No
Because all I'll ever be
Is a GHOST

www.ingramcontent.com/pod-product-compliance
Lightning Source LLC
Chambersburg PA
CBHW062008040426
42447CB00010B/1968